C000183181

by Iain Gray

Lang**Syne**

PUBLISHING

WRITING *to* REMEMBER

LangSyne

PUBLISHING

WRITING *to* REMEMBER

79 Main Street, Newtongrange,
Midlothian EH22 4NA
Tel: 0131 344 0414   Fax: 0845 075 6085
E-mail: info@lang-syne.co.uk
www.langsyneshop.co.uk

Design by Dorothy Meikle
Printed by Ricoh Print Scotland
© Lang Syne Publishers Ltd 2015

ISBN 978-1-85217-664-8

John

MOTTO:
God feeds the ravens.

CREST:
Two crossed battle axes.

NAME variations include:
John
Johne
Johns

Chapter one:

Origins of Welsh surnames

by Iain Gray

If you don't know where you came from, you won't know where you're going **is a frequently quoted observation and one that has a particular resonance today when there has been a marked upsurge in interest in genealogy, with increasing numbers of people curious to trace their family roots.**

Main sources for genealogical research include census returns and official records of births, marriages and deaths – and the key to unlocking the detail they contain is obviously a family surname, one that has been 'inherited' and passed from generation to generation.

No matter our station in life, we all have a surname – but it was not until about the middle of the fourteenth century that the practice of being identified by a particular, or 'fixed', surname became commonly established throughout the British Isles.

Previous to this, it was normal for a person to be identified through the use of only a forename.

Wales, however, known in the Welsh language as *Cymru*, is uniquely different – with the use of what are known as patronymic names continuing well into the fifteenth century and, in remote rural areas, up until the early nineteenth century.

Patronymic names are ones where a son takes his father's forename, or Christian name, as his surname.

Examples of patronymic names throughout the British Isles include 'Johnson', indicating 'son of John', while specifically in Scotland 'son of' was denoted by the prefix Mc or Mac – with 'MacDonald', for example, meaning 'son of Donald.'

Early Welsh law, known as *Cyfraith Hywel*, *The Law of Hywel*, introduced by Hywel the Good, who ruled from Prestatyn to Pembroke between 915 AD and 950 AD, stipulated that a person's name should indicate their ancestry – the name in effect being a type of 'family tree.'

This required the prefixes *ap* or *ab* – derived from *mab*, meaning 'son of' being placed before the person's baptismal name.

In the case of females, the suffixes *verch* or *ferch*, sometimes shortened to *vch* or *vz* would be attached to their Christian name to indicate 'daughter of.'

In some cases, rather than being known for

example as *Llewellyn ap Thomas – Llewellyn son of Thomas* – Llewellyn's name would incorporate an 'ancestral tree' going back much earlier than his father.

One source gives the example of *Llewellyn ap Thomas ap Dafydd ap Evan ap Owen ap John* – meaning *Llewellyn son of Thomas son of Dafydd son of Evan son of Owen son of John*.

This leads to great confusion, to say the least, when trying to trace a person's ancestry back to a particular family – with many people having the forenames, for example, of Llewellyn, Thomas, Owen or John.

The first Act of Union between Wales and England that took place in 1536 during the reign of Henry VIII required that all Welsh names be registered in an Anglicised form – with *Hywel*, for example, becoming Howell, or Powell, and *Gruffydd* becoming Griffiths.

An early historical example of this concerns William ap John Thomas, standard bearer to Henry VIII, who became William Jones.

In many cases – as in Davies and Williams – an s was simply added to the original patronymic name, while in other cases the prefix *ap* or *ab* was contracted to *p* or *b* to prefix the name – as in *ab Evan* to form Bevan and *ap Richard* to form Pritchard.

Other original Welsh surnames – such as Morgan, originally *Morcant* – derive from ancient Celtic sources, while others stem from a person's physical characteristics – as in *Gwyn* or *Wynne* a nickname for someone with fair hair, *Gough* or *Gooch* denoting someone with red hair or a ruddy complexion, *Gethin* indicating swarthy or ugly and *Lloyd* someone with brown or grey hair.

With many popular surnames found today in Wales being based on popular Christian names such as John, this means that what is known as the 'stock' or 'pool' of names is comparatively small compared to that of common surnames found in England, Scotland and Ireland.

This explains why, in a typical Welsh village or town with many bearers of a particular name not necessarily being related, they were differentiated by being known, for example, as 'Jones the butcher', 'Jones the teacher' and 'Jones the grocer.'

Another common practice, dating from about the nineteenth century, was to differentiate among families of the same name by prefixing it with the mother's surname or hyphenating the name.

The history of the origins and development of Welsh surnames is inextricably bound up with the nation's frequently turbulent history and its rich culture.

Speaking a Celtic language known as Brythonic, which would gradually evolve into Welsh, the natives were subjected to Roman invasion in 48 AD, and in the following centuries to invasion by the Anglo-Saxons, Vikings and Normans.

Under England's ruthless and ambitious Edward I, the nation was fortified with castles between 1276 and 1295 to keep the 'rebellious' natives in check – but this did not prevent a series of bloody uprisings against English rule that included, most notably, Owain Glyndŵr's rebellion in 1400.

Politically united with England through the first Act of Union in 1536, becoming part of the Kingdom of Great Britain in 1707 and part of the United Kingdom in 1801, it was in 1999 that *Cynulliad Cenedlaethol Cymru*, the National Assembly for Wales, was officially opened by the Queen.

Welsh language and literature has flourished throughout the nation's long history.

In what is known as the Heroic Age, early Welsh poets include the late sixth century Taliesin and Aneirin, author of *Y Gododdin*.

Discovered in a thirteenth century manuscript but thought to date from anywhere between the seventh and eleventh centuries, it refers to the kingdom of Gododdin that took in south-east Scotland and

Northumberland and was part of what was once the Welsh territory known as *Hen Ogledd*, *The Old North*.

Commemorating Gododdin warriors who were killed in battle against the Angles of Bernicia and Deira at Catraith in about 600 AD, the manuscript – known as *Llyfr Aneirin*, *Book of Aneirin* – is now in the precious care of Cardiff City Library.

Other important early works by Welsh poets include the fourteenth century *Red Book of Hergest*, now held in the Bodleian Library, Oxford, and the *White Book of Rhydderch*, kept in the National Library of Wales, Aberystwyth.

William Morgan's translation of the Bible into Welsh in 1588 is hailed as having played an important role in the advancement of the Welsh language, while in I885 Dan Isaac Davies founded the first Welsh language society.

It was in 1856 that Evan James and his son James James composed the rousing Welsh national anthem *Hen Wlad Fynhadad – Land of My Fathers*, while in the twentieth century the poet Dylan Thomas gained international fame and acclaim with poems such as *Under Milk Wood*.

The nation's proud cultural heritage is also celebrated through *Eisteddfod Genedlaethol Cymru*, the National Eisteddfod of Wales, the annual festival of music, literature and performance that is held across the nation and which traces its roots back to 1176 when Rhys ap Gruffyd, who ruled the territory of Deheubarth from 1155 to 1197, hosted a magnificent festival of poetry and song at his court in Cardigan.

The 2011 census for Wales unfortunately shows that the number of people able to speak the language has declined from 20.8% of the population of just under 3.1 million in 2001 to 19% – but overall the nation's proud culture, reflected in its surnames, still flourishes.

Many Welsh families proudly boast the heraldic device known as a Coat of Arms, as featured on our front cover.

The central motif of the Coat of Arms would originally have been what was borne on the shield of a warrior to distinguish himself from others on the battlefield.

Not featured on the Coat of Arms, but highlighted on page three, is the family motto and related crest – with the latter frequently different from the central motif.

Echoes of a far distant past can still be found in our surnames and they can be borne with pride in commemoration of our forebears.

Chapter two:

Invasion and conquest

A popular forename in addition to a surname, 'John' is of truly Biblical roots, derived as it is from the Hebrew 'Yochanan', indicating 'He who Jehovah has favoured (with a son)', or 'Graced by God.'

Although also popularised as a forename through reverence for John the Baptist and John the Evangelist, or John the Divine, it developed as a surname, in common with many others, in the decades following the Norman Conquest of 1066 – with some sources asserting it was introduced to Europe by returning Christian Crusaders.

In Wales, meanwhile, another possible point of origin of the name is from the bardic 'Ieuanc', indicating 'young', while its patronymic form of 'ap John' denotes 'son of John.'

What was to eventually prove to be the death knell of Welsh independence was sounded by the Norman Conquest.

A key date in not only English but also Welsh history, by 1066 England had become a nation with several powerful competitors to the throne.

In what were extremely complex family,

political and military machinations, the monarch was Harold II, who had succeeded to the throne following the death of Edward the Confessor.

But his right to the crown was contested by two powerful competitors – his brother-in-law King Harold Hardrada of Norway, in alliance with Tostig, Harold II's brother, and Duke William II of Normandy.

On October 14, Harold II encountered a mighty invasion force, led by Duke William, that had landed at Hastings, in East Sussex.

Harold drew up a strong defensive position, at the top of Senlac Hill, building a shield wall to repel William's cavalry and infantry.

The Normans suffered heavy losses, but through a combination of the deadly skill of their archers and the ferocious determination of their cavalry they eventually won the day.

Anglo-Saxon morale had collapsed on the battlefield as word spread through the ranks that Harold, the last of the Anglo-Saxon kings, had been killed.

William was declared King of England on December 25, and the complete subjugation of his Anglo-Saxon subjects followed, with those Normans who had fought on his behalf rewarded with lands – a pattern that would be repeated in Wales.

Invading across the Welsh Marches, the

borderland between England and Wales, the Normans gradually consolidated gains by building castles, but under a succession of Welsh leaders resistance proved strong.

However, it was brutally crushed in 1283 under England's ruthless and ambitious Edward I, who ordered the building or repair of at least 17 castles and in 1302 proclaiming his son and heir, the future Edward II, as Prince of Wales, a title known in Welsh as *Tywysog Cymru*.

A heroic Welsh figure arose from 1400 to 1415 in the form of Owain Glyndŵr – the last native Welshman to be recognised by his supporters as *Tywysog Cymru*.

In what is known as The Welsh Revolt he achieved an early series of stunning victories against Henry IV and his successor Henry V – until mysteriously disappearing from the historical record after mounting an ambush in Brecon.

Some sources assert that he was either killed in the ambush or died a short time afterwards from wounds he received – but there is a persistent tradition that he survived and lived thereafter in anonymity, protected by loyal followers.

During the revolt, he had consistently refused offers of a Royal Pardon and – despite offers of hefty rewards for his capture – he was never betrayed.

Those who would come to bear the John surname feature prominently in the frequently turbulent historical record, while early bearers were particularly associated with Carmarthenshire, in the south west of Wales, and known in Welsh as *Sir Gaerfyddin* or *Sir Gar* and with 'Sir' denoting 'County'.

During the tumultuous seventeenth century, John ap John, known in Welsh as Sion ap Sion and born in about 1625 at Pen-y-cefn, North Wales, is better known to posterity as 'The Apostle of the Quakers in Wales.'

During the Interregnum, or Commonwealth – the period between the execution of Charles I in 1649 and the Restoration of his successor Charles II in 1660, John ap John had for a time been an adherent of Puritanism – the doctrine that abhorred elaborate forms of religious worship and favoured a strict morality that was reflected in non-ostentatious forms of dress.

A member of the Puritan congregation at Wrexham, it was in 1653 that John ap John travelled to Swarthmore, Lancashire, to meet George Fox, founder of the religious grouping known as The Friends of Truth, nicknamed Quakers after Fox had told a judge to "tremble at the name of the Lord."

Converted to the Quaker faith by Fox, John ap John set about to zealously evangelise throughout his native Wales, frequently being thrown into prison for his pains, but gathering significant numbers of converts in the process.

Rejecting a professional ministry and refusing to pay tithes or swear oaths to the Established Church, the Quakers were subjected to persecution and many found refuge in Pennsylvania, which William Penn had founded as a Quaker colony in 1682.

Many Welsh Quakers left their homeland for Pennsylvania, but John ap John remained.

Following the death of his wife Katrin in 1695, he went to live with his daughter and her husband in Stafford, and it was here that he died two years later.

A leading member of the working class movement known as Chartism – that sought political equality and social justice – David John was the Unitarian Church minister and blacksmith by trade born in 1782 in St Clears, on the River Taf, Carmarthenshire.

Appointed minister of a chapel at Twynyrodyn, Merthyr Tydfil, in 1826 and with the Chartist movement perceived by some as dangerously revolutionary, threatening the established order, David John's activities led to his congregation dispersing and the closure of the chapel.

Undaunted, he set up a small school for workmen near his smithy in Merthyr Tydfil.

He died in 1853, while his sons David and Matthew were also prominent figures in the Chartist movement – with David John co-publisher from 1840 to 1842 of the Welsh Chartist paper *Udgorn Cymru* and the *Advocate and Merthyr Free Press*.

Pursuing a more conventional form of politics, Brynmor John, born in 1934 in Treforest, Pontypridd, the son of a painter and decorator, was the Welsh Labour Party politician who, after being elected Member of Parliament (MP) for Pontypridd in 1970 went on to serve in high office.

These posts included, from 1976 to 1979, Minister of State at the Home Office and, from 1981 to 1983, Opposition Spokesman on Social Services.

Chairman of the Welsh Labour Group from 1983 to 1984, he died in 1988.

Chapter three:

Art for art's sake

One remarkable family of the proud name of John is one that boasted not only renowned artists but also an influential twentieth century Royal Navy officer.

They were the Welsh painter Augustus John, his sister Gwendolen John, better known as Gwen John, his wife Ida, neé Nettleship, and his son Sir Caspar John who, after distinguished service during the Second World War, held the powerful post of First Sea Lord.

Born in 1878 in Tenby, Pembrokeshire, the son of a solicitor and the third of four sons, Augustus Edward John was aged six when his mother Augusta died – after having aroused a passion for drawing in her son and her daughter Gwen.

Aged seventeen when he enrolled at the Tenby School of Art, Augustus John studied a short time later at the Slade School of Art, London, sharing lodgings with his sister who was also studying there and existing on a frugal diet of nuts and fruit.

Even before his graduation his drawing teacher Henry Tonks had recognised him as 'the most talented draughtsman of his generation.'

Winning the prestigious Slade Prize in 1897 for

his *Moses and the Brazen Serpent*, John studied for a time in Paris before taking up a post teaching art at the University of Liverpool.

Having married the artist Ida Nettleship in 1900, he later spent two years in his native Wales along with his student James Dickson Innes painting in the Arenig Valley, Snowdonia, in particular the brooding majesty of the mountain of Arenig Fawr.

In 2011, this period in the Arenig Valley became the subject of the BBC documentary *The Mountain that Had to Be Painted*.

Moving to Provence and captivated by its light, John painted there from 1910 to 1928 and, in keeping with is rather Bohemian lifestyle – living in a ménage à trois with his wife and his mistress Dorothy (Dorelia) McNeill – he developed an interest in the Romani people.

So great was this interest that he was appointed president of the Gypsy Lore Society in 1937, serving in the post until his death.

During the carnage of the First World War, he was attached as a war artist to the Canadian forces serving on the Western Front – but after only two months he was sent back to Britain in disgrace after taking part in a rather unseemly brawl that in all probability had been fuelled by copious amounts of alcohol.

Through the intervention of the Canadian-born newspaper tycoon Lord Beaverbrook, he escaped a court martial while Beaverbrook also used his considerable influence for him to plan a proposed Canadian War Memorial painting.

It was not until 2011 that the result of this work, *The Canadians Opposite Lens*, was unveiled at the Canadian War Museum, in Ottawa.

Famed for his drawings, etchings and paintings, John was also equally in demand for his portraiture work – executing portraits of celebrities of his time who included T.E. Lawrence, better known as Lawrence of Arabia, the actress Tallulah Bankhead, the novelist Thomas Hardy, the playwright George Bernard Shaw and the poets W.B. Yeats and Dylan Thomas.

Author of two volumes of autobiography, the 1952 *Chiaroscuro* and, from 1964, *Finishing Touches*, he continued to work from his home in Fordingbridge, Hampshire, until his death in 1961.

Elected to the Royal Academy in 1921, named to the Order of Merit in 1942, a trustee of the Tate Gallery from 1933 to 1941 and president for a time of the Royal Society of Portrait Painters, he is the subject of the 1944 Joyce Cary novel *The Horse's Mouth*, adapted for a film of the name in 1958 and starring Alec Guinness in the role of John.

Described by her admirers as 'a Bohemian-style icon', his older sister Gwen John, born in 1876, had studied at the Slade School of Art at a time when it was the only one in Britain that admitted female students.

Also studying figure drawing under her brother's early mentor Henry Tonks, she visited Paris in 1898 and studied under James McNeill Whistler, while from 1900 to 1901 she lived as a squatter in a derelict building in London – such were her precarious financial circumstances.

Back in France by 1903 and accompanied for a time by her brother's mistress and future second wife Dorelia McNeill, she subsisted by selling portrait sketches and working as an artists' model – including the sculptor Auguste Rodin, and becoming his lover.

But so intense was her attachment to him, that he was forced to end the relationship and use a small army of secretaries and other assistants to keep her away from him.

Her financial circumstances improved greatly in 1911 when the wealthy American art collector John Quinn became her patron, buying up the bulk of the work she produced until his death in 1924.

With paintings that include *The Convalescent*, *Young Woman in a Spotted Blue Dress* and *Girl Holding a Cat*, she died in 1939 – while some of her work is now in the collections of the National Museum, Cardiff and the Tate Britain, London.

Her sister-in-law Ida Nettleship, Augustus Johns' first wife, born in 1877 in Hampstead, London, also studied at the Slade School of Art and, for a time, under Whistler.

It was two years after her marriage that her husband met Dorelia McNeill and such was the mutual affectation among the three that she appears to have been quite content to share her husband with her.

She died in 1907, having had five sons by him.

Augustus John later married Doleria, who bore him five children, while one of Augustus and Ida's sons found fame in a field totally unrelated to that of art.

Born in 1903, Caspar John, later more formally known as Admiral of the Fleet Sir Caspar John, was aged only thirteen when – initially against his father's wishes but with his stepmother Dorelia's support – he entered the Royal Navy College, Osborne, on the Isle of Wight.

In later years he recalled that his interest in a life at sea had first been sparked when, aged nine, he was presented with a copy of *Jane's Fighting Ships* after winning the prize for 'best gentleman in school.'

Promoted to midshipman in 1921 and serving

in the Mediterranean Fleet, he later qualified as a pilot in the Fleet Air Arm and became one of its early pioneers.

Serving on aircraft carriers and cruisers during the 1930s, he served for a time during the Second World War on Atlantic convoy escort duties, having been promoted to captain in 1941.

Appointed director-general of naval aircraft production at the Ministry of Aircraft Production and, in 1943, naval air attaché at the British Embassy in Washington, three years after the conflict ended in 1945 he was placed in command of the Royal Naval Air Station, Lossiemouth.

Promoted to full admiral in 1957 and honoured in the same year as a Knight Commander of the Order of the Bath, he was appointed First Sea Lord and Chief of the Naval Staff in 1960, serving in the post until he retired in 1963.

The public figurehead for the Industrial Society's "I'm Backing Britain" campaign in 1968 and chairman of the Back Pain Association, he died in 1984.

Chapter four:

On the world stage

Bearers of the John name and its popular spelling variation of Johns have achieved international success and celebrity.

One of the world's top-selling popular music artists, Reginald Kenneth Dwight is the multi-award-winning English singer, songwriter, composer, pianist and record producer better known as **Elton John** and more formally as Sir Elton John.

Born in 1947 in Pinner, Middlesex, the son of a flight lieutenant in the RAF, he was a musical prodigy, starting to learn to play the piano at the tender age of only three while eight years later he won a junior scholarship to the Royal Academy of Music.

Taking to the stage when he was aged fifteen and billed as "Reggie", he played piano at weekends in a local hotel, while two years later he and some friends formed a band called Bluesology.

His big break came in 1967 when, along with budding lyricist Bernie Taupin, he responded to an advertisement for songwriters placed in *New Musical Express* by Liberty Records.

The pair, who had never previously met, were

teamed up – forging one of the most successful songwriting partnerships in the history of popular music.

Joining Dick James' DJM Records a year later as staff songwriters and with 'Reggie' now having adopted the name 'Elton John' – in recognition of his admiration for the blues musicians Elton Dean and Long John Baldry – he and Taupin penned a number of songs for other artists, while Elton also worked as a session musician.

It is his piano work, for example, that features on The Hollies 1969 hit *He Ain't Heavy, He's my Brother*.

Success in their own right came in 1969 with the debut album *Empty Sky*, followed a year later with the self-titled *Elton John*.

Further international success followed over the years with a string of best-selling singles and albums including *Your Song*, *Crocodile Rock*, *Daniel*, *Goodbye Yellow Brick Road*, *Bennie and the Jets*, *Candle in the Wind* and *Saturday Night's Alright for Fighting*.

Renowned for his 'glam rock' stage extravaganzas, Elton John also pursued a different musical path through his collaboration with lyricist Tim Rice – writing the songs for the 1994 Disney animated film *The Lion King*, with the track *Can You Feel the Love Tonight* winner of the Academy Award for Best Song.

Following the death of Diana, Princess of Wales in 1997, he asked Bernie Taupin to revise his lyrics for their 1973 *Candle in the Wind* – originally written in homage to Marilyn Monroe.

It was this revised version, with the opening lyrics "Goodbye, England's rose …" that he performed at her funeral in Westminster Abbey.

With all proceeds from the song donated to the Diana, Princess of Wales Memorial Fund, it is the best-selling single in both UK and American Billboard chart history.

After entering into a civil partnership with the filmmaker David Furnish in 2005, the couple married in December of 2014 after gay marriage was legalised in England, while he has also raised substantial amounts for the fight against AIDS through his Elton John AIDS Foundation.

The recipient of a host of honours and awards that include six Grammy Awards, five Brit Awards, induction – along with Bernie Taupin – into the Songwriters' Hall of Fame, a star on the Hollywood Walk of Fame and a CBE, he received the accolade of knighthood in 1998 in recognition of his charitable work.

Co-star along with John Travolta in the highly successful 1978 film adaptation of the Broadway

musical *Grease*, **Olivia Newton-John** is the British-born
Australian singer and actress who is the recipient of four
Grammy Awards.

Born in Cambridge in 1948, her family
background is no less interesting than her own career.

Her Welsh-born father Bryn Newton-John was
an MI5 officer during the Second World War involved
with the highly-secret decoding of German signals
traffic at Bletchley Park, while he was also tasked with
taking Hitler's deputy Rudolf Hess into custody when he
mysteriously arrived in Britain in May of 1941, ostensibly
on a peace mission.

Her mother, Irene, meanwhile, was a daughter
of the German Nobel Prize-winning atomic physicist
Max Born, who fled to Britain to escape Nazi persecution
of the Jews.

Immigrating with her family to Australia when
she was aged six, settling in Melbourne, she was aged
fourteen when she formed an all-girl group and later
became a regular performer on radio and television.

Recording her first solo single, *Till You Say
You'll Be Mine* in 1966, she went on to enjoy a
succession of hits that include *If Not For You* and *Banks
of the Ohio*, while in 1974 she represented Britain in
the Eurovision Song Contest – being placed fourth with
Long Live Love.

But it was in the lead role of Sandy in *Grease* that she achieved even greater fame and success.

The biggest box-office hit of 1978, the soundtrack album provided her with no fewer than three hit singles – *You're The One That I Want*, *Summer Nights* and *Hopelessly Devoted to You*.

An activist for animal rights and environmental issues, she is also a leading advocate for health awareness, having survived breast cancer in 1992, while in 2008 she took part in a BBC Wales programme, *Coming Home*, about her Welsh family background through her father.

In the genres of rhythm and blues and rock and roll, William Edward John, better known as **Little Willie John** and also as LWJ, was born in 1937 in Cullendale, Arkansas.

One of ten children, he was aged four when his family moved to Detroit, and he later took to the stage as part of a gospel singing group and performed on talent shows.

Talent-spotted and signed to a recording deal in 1955, he went on to have a string of hits that include *All Around the World*, *Need Your Love So Bad* and *Fever* – the latter also a major hit for Peggy Lee.

Despite his great success, his record company was forced to drop him in 1963 because of his alcohol abuse and erratic behaviour – and he was convicted three years later for a fatal stabbing incident following a show in Seattle.

The deeply troubled musician died in Washington State Penitentiary in 1968 and, eighteen years later, was posthumously inducted into the Rock and Roll Hall of Fame.

One of his sisters, **Mable John**, is the blues vocalist who in 1960 became one of the first acts to be signed to the famed Tamla Motown label; born in 1930, she has had hits that include *Who Wouldn't Love a Man Like That?* and *Your Good Thing Is About to End*.

In the recording studio, **Glyn Johns** is the legendary engineer and producer who has worked with an impressive list of artists from the 1960s until the present day who include the Rolling Stones, The Who, Led Zeppelin, Bob Dylan, Emmylou Harris and the Eagles.

Born in 1942 in Epsom, Surrey and an inductee of the Rock and Roll Hall of Fame, he is the older brother of the late sound engineer and record producer **Andy John**, who worked on albums that include the Rolling Stones' 1972 *Exile on Main Street* and other artists who include Rod Stewart.

Born in 1950, he died in 2013, while he was the father of the engineer, producer, songwriter and multi-instrumentalist **Ethan Johns**.

Born in 1969 in Merton, Surrey and the recipient of the 2012 Brit Award for Best British Producer, he has worked for a range of artists who include Paul McCartney, Tom Jones, Kings of Leon, Crosby, Stills and Nash and Kaiser Chiefs.

His brother, **Will Johns**, born in 1973, is the blues and rock singer and guitarist who has performed with artists who include Jack Bruce, Bill Wyman and Ronnie Wood.

Bearers of the John name have also excelled in the highly competitive world of sport – not least in the rough and tumble that is the game of rugby.

Capped nineteen times for Wales, Ernest Raymond John, better known as **Roy John**, was the rugby union lock born in 1925 in Crynant, Dulais Valley, and who died in 1981.

Playing club rugby for Crynant and Neath, his international debut was against England as part of the 1950 Five Nations Championship.

Selected for that year's British Lions Tour to Australia and New Zealand, he was also a member of the two Grand Slam-winning teams – in 1950 and 1952.

Playing during what is known as the amateur era of the game in the 1960s and early 1970s, **Barry John** is the Welsh former rugby union fly-half born in 1945 in Cefneithin, in the early John heartland of Carmarthenshire.

The recipient of 25 caps for the Wales national team and five for the British Lions and part of the winning Welsh side in the 1971 Five Nations Championship, he played club rugby for Cefneithin and Llanelli.

From sport to the stage, **Caroline John** was the English actress of theatre, television and film best known for her role of Liz Shaw in the science fiction series *Doctor Who*.

Born in York in 1940, she appeared in the series in 1970 beside Jon Pertwee as the doctor's companion, while as a stage actress she toured with the Royal Shakespeare Company and the National Theatre in acclaimed productions that include *Juno and the Paycock*, *The Merchant of Venice* and *Much Ado About Nothing*.

With big screen credits that include the 1973 *The Assassin*, the 1997 *The Woodlanders* and, from 2003, *Love Actually*, she died in 2012.

Of Welsh roots, **Glynis Johns** is the award-winning British actress born in 1923 in Pretoria, South Africa.

One of her best known roles is that of Desiree Armfeldt in the 1973 Broadway production of *A Little*

Night Music, in which she sang the Stephen Sondheim composition *Send in the Clowns*.

Her performance won her a Tony Award, while notable film credits include the 1960 *The Sundowners*, for which she received an Academy Award nomination for Best Actress, the 1964 *Mary Poppins*, the 1972 *Under Milk Wood* and, from 1999, *Superstar*.

From the stage to the creative world of the written word, one particularly colourful bearer of the Johns name was William Earl Johns, better known by his pen-name of **Captain W.E. Johns**.

Creator of the *Biggles* series of adventures featuring the daredevil pilot, adventurer and defender of the British Empire James Bigglesworth, better known as Biggles, he was born in 1893 in Bengeo, Hereford, and worked for a time as a sanitary inspector before being commissioned into the Royal Flying Corps (RFC), forerunner of the RAF, during the First World War.

A flying instructor at one stage in the conflict, he achieved the unenviable distinction of writing off three aircraft in the space of three days through engine failure.

One crashed into the sea, one onto a beach and the other through the back door of a fellow officer's home.

I n September of 1918, piloting one of a group

of six De Havilland DH4s tasked with bombing the German city of Mannheim, he was shot down; his co-pilot died of his injuries, while Johns spent the remainder of the war as a prisoner.

Choosing the pen-name 'Captain' W.E. Johns – although he never attained this rank – he wrote his first *Biggles* book, *The White Fokker*, in 1932, and continued writing the adventurers right up until his death in 1968.